Jamaican Cookbook:

Traditional Jamaican Recipes Made Easy

information is without a contract or any type of guarantee assurance.

The trademarks that are used are without any consent, and the publication of the trademark is without permission or backing by the trademark owner. All trademarks and brands within this book are for clarifying purposes only and are the owned by the owners themselves, not affiliated with this document.

GRIZZLY PUBLISHING

WWW.GRIZZLYPUBLISHING.COM

Table of Contents

Introduction

First of all, I would love to thank you for purchasing this book, "Jamaican Cookbook: Traditional Jamaican Recipes Made Easy" and I assure you that you have made the right choice in doing so.

You may have shown some interest in the Jamaican style of cooking or the traditional way the cuisine is prepared in and you most probably hit a lot of dead-ends while trying to figure out simple ways to try these exquisite traditional recipes. It's possible you have also seen Jamaican food being prepared on television or doing its rounds on social media, but you could never gather the courage to take the plunge into preparing some amazing Jamaican food yourself.

If these have been the cases you relate to even in the slightest – this book is here to prove it that yes! Traditional Jamaican cooking *can* be achieved in anyone's kitchen, without much hassle.

Some of the best and most amazing traditional Jamaican recipes have been compiled and crafted into this book for you to further your interest in Jamaican cuisine and turn it into a fully-fledged culinary passion your friends and family are going to fawn over the taste of.

What are you waiting for? Read on and discover flavorsome chapters that just might entice you into entering the kitchen long before you are done with this book!

Thank you!

Chapter One: Breakfast

Cornmeal Porridge

Makes: 2 servings

Ingredients

- ½ cup fine yellow cornmeal
- ½ cup milk
- Sugar to taste or fat free condensed milk
- 1/8 teaspoon ground cinnamon
- ½ teaspoon vanilla extract
- 1 ½ cups water
- 1/8 teaspoon ground nutmeg

Method

1. Add cornmeal and ½ cup water into a bowl and mix well.
2. Pour milk and remaining water into a saucepan. Place the saucepan over medium heat.
3. When it begins to boil, add cornmeal mixture and salt. Stir constantly.
4. Lower heat and simmer for 5-6 minutes.
5. Add rest of the ingredients and stir.
6. Ladle into bowls.
7. Serve it hot.

Callaloo and Saltfish

It's a popular breakfast dish for the weekends

Makes: 4

Ingredients

- 1 ½ pounds callaloo leaves, rinsed, chopped
- 2 sprigs thyme
- ¾ pound saltfish (cod fish)
- 1 crushed garlic or 3 teaspoons garlic powder
- 1 ½ scotch bonnet peppers
- Pepper to taste
- 1/3 cup water
- 1 ½ tablespoons margarine or vegetable oil
- 1 large onion, chopped
- Salt to taste

Method

1. Place a skillet or nonstick pan over medium heat. Add oil. When the oil is heated, add saltfish, garlic, thyme, onion and pepper and sauté until onions are translucent.
2. Add callaloo leaves and water and mix.
3. Cover with a lid and cook until tender.
4. Add scotch bonnet pepper, salt and pepper. Simmer for a few minutes.
5. Serving options: Pear slices / Avocado slices / boiled banana / fried dumplings

Scrambled Eggs with Tomatoes

Makes: 6 servings

Ingredients

- 12 eggs
- 2 tablespoons butter
- ½ cup green tomato, chopped
- 1 teaspoon basil, chopped
- 4 teaspoons tomato paste
- ½ cup red tomato, diced
- Salt to taste
- Pepper to taste
- 4 teaspoons chili sauce

Method

1. Add eggs into a bowl. Whisk well. Add chili sauce and tomato paste and whisk until well combined.
2. Place a skillet over medium heat. Add butter. When butter melts, add eggs. Stir frequently and scramble the eggs.
3. When the eggs are half cooked, add tomatoes, salt, pepper and basil. Mix well.
4. Cook until the eggs are done.
5. Serve hot.

Rice Porridge

Makes: 2 -3 servings

Ingredients

- ¾ cup rice, rinsed
- ¼ cup sweetened condensed milk
- ¼ cup flour
- ½ cup milk
- 1/8 teaspoon ground cinnamon
- Sugar to taste
- 2 ½ cups water
- ¼ teaspoon ground nutmeg
- 1/8 teaspoon vanilla extract (optional)
- ¼ teaspoon salt

Method

1. Add rice, milk, sugar, 2 cups water and salt into a saucepan.
2. Place the saucepan over medium heat.
3. When it begins to boil lower heat and simmer until rice is cooked.
4. Add flour and remaining water into a bowl and stir well. Pour into the saucepan. Stir occasionally.
5. Add rest of the ingredients and stir.
6. Ladle into bowls.
7. Serve it hot.

Vegan Rice Porridge

Makes: 2 servings

Ingredients

- ½ cup brown rice, rinsed
- ½ jar coconut condensed milk
- 2 tablespoons coconut milk (optional)
- ¾ - 1 cup almond milk
- ½ teaspoon ground cinnamon
- 1 ¾ cups water
- ½ teaspoon ground nutmeg
- ½ teaspoon vanilla extract
- 1/8 teaspoon Himalayan pink salt

Method

1. Add rice into a bowl. Pour lukewarm water into it. Add ½ tablespoon lime juice. Cover and let it soak for 7-8 hours.
2. Drain the water and rinse many times.
3. Add rice and water into a saucepan.
4. Place the saucepan over medium heat.
5. When it begins to boil, lower heat and simmer until rice is cooked. Add more water if required. It should not be very dry. When rice is cooked, at least 2-3 tablespoons of water should be remaining in the pan. If not, add a little water.
6. Add rest of the ingredients and stir. Let simmer for a few minutes. Stir frequently.
7. Ladle into bowls.
8. Serve it hot.

Banana Bread

Makes: 8 servings of 1 slice

Ingredients

- 1 tablespoon + 1 teaspoon butter, softened
- ½ cup sugar
- 4.5 ounces all-purpose flour
- ¼ teaspoon baking soda
- 1 teaspoon baking powder
- ½ cup mashed ripe banana
- 1 tablespoon dark rum or 1/8 teaspoon imitation rum extract
- 1 teaspoon lime juice
- 2 tablespoons toasted chopped pecans
- 2 tablespoons packed brown sugar
- 1 tablespoon light cream cheese, softened
- 1 small egg
- A pinch salt
- ¼ cup fat free milk
- ¼ teaspoon lime rind, grated
- 2 tablespoons flaked coconut, sweetened
- Cooking spray

For frosting:

- 1 teaspoon butter
- 1 teaspoon lime juice
- 1 teaspoon dark rum
- 1 tablespoon pecans, chopped, toasted
- 1 tablespoons shredded coconut, sweetened

Method

1. Grease a small loaf pan with cooking spray.
2. Add 1-tablespoon butter and cream cheese into a mixing bowl. Beat on medium speed until well combined.
3. Beat in sugar and egg.
4. Add flour, baking soda, baking powder and salt into a bowl and stir. Set aside.
5. Add rest of the ingredients (except pecans and coconut) into another bowl and whisk until well combined.
6. Add the banana mixture with the flour mix, alternately, a little at a time into the bowl of butter – cream mixture. Mix well each time.
7. Add coconut and pecans and fold gently.
8. Pour into the prepared loaf pan.
9. Bake in a preheated oven 375° F for 40-45 minutes or until a knife when inserted at the center of the bread comes out clean.
10. To make frosting: Add butter, lime juice and rum into a small saucepan.
11. Place the saucepan over medium heat. Stirring constantly cook for 50-60 seconds.
12. Add pecans and coconut and turn off the heat.
13. Spread over the banana bread.

Fish Fritters

This can also be served as an appetizer.

Makes: 2 servings

- ½ pound dried saltfish (cod fish)
- 1 tablespoon baking powder
- ½ teaspoon paprika
- ½ teaspoon salt
- 2 stalks scallions, finely chopped
- ¼ scotch bonnet pepper, finely chopped
- 1 cup flour
- 1 small clove garlic, minced
- Pepper to taste
- 1 medium onion, finely chopped
- 1 large tomato, finely chopped
- ¼ cup water or more if required
- Oil, as required

Method:

1. Soak the saltfish overnight or for about 8 hours by submerging it in cold water in order to remove the excess salt. Throughout this time period, drain out the water and add fresh water a few times.
2. Pat the saltfish dry by patting with paper towels or a clean kitchen towel.
3. Finely shred the saltfish and place in a bowl. Set aside.
4. Place a skillet over medium heat. Add a little oil. When the oil is heated, add garlic, onion, scallion, tomato and bonnet pepper and sauté for 2-3 minutes. Turn off the heat.

5. Add all the dry ingredients into a bowl and stir. Add into the bowl of saltfish. Add water and mix until well combined.
6. Add the sautéed vegetables and mix well.
7. Place a small deep pan over medium heat. Add about a cup of oil. When the oil is well heated, but not smoking, drop spoonfuls of the batter in the oil.
8. Fry until the fritters are golden brown. Fry in batches. Remove the fritters and place on a plate lined with paper towels.
9. Serve right away.

Ackee and Saltfish

Makes: 2 servings

Ingredients

- 4 ounces of saltfish – salted codfish, dried
- 1 small onion
- ½ of 1 18 ounces can of ackees, drained (or 6 fresh ackees)
- ¼ teaspoon of black pepper
- ¼ of hot pepper
- 1 ½ tablespoon of butter
- ½ of sweet pepper
- ½ teaspoon of dried thyme
- ½ tomato, chopped
- Optional – 2 spring onions
- Optional - 2 cloves of garlic
- Optional - 3 slices of bacon

Method

1. Soak the saltfish overnight or for about 8 hours by submerging it in cold water in order to remove the excess salt. Throughout this time period, drain out the water and add fresh water a few times.
2. Add some cold water to a pan and bring it to a boil over high heat. Once it starts boiling, bring the heat down to low medium and add in the saltfish. Allow it to simmer gently for about 20 minutes or until the fish is tender.
3. Chop the sweet pepper, hot pepper, onion, and tomato.

4. Take the saltfish out of the water and let it cool down. Once it has cooled down, using your fingers, de-bone the fish and flake it apart.
5. Take a frying pan and melt the butter in it, add in the onion, sweet pepper, thyme, and hot pepper for around 2 minutes.
6. Chuck in the flaked fish and tomatoes and let it cook for 10 more minutes.
7. Lastly, add in the ackee and let it cook until the ackee has heated through. Be gentle while stirring to prevent the ackee from breaking apart.
8. Serve hot with boiled green banana, yam, and fried dumplings (Johnnycakes).
9. Enjoy!

Green Banana Porridge

Makes: 2

Ingredients

- 2-3 green bananas, unripe and firm
- ½ cup of water
- ½ cup plus ½ cup of milk (or use ¼ cup of coconut milk)
- ½ teaspoon of cinnamon powder
- 1/8 teaspoon of allspice
- ¼ teaspoon of nutmeg
- ½ cup condensed milk, sweetened
- ½ teaspoon of vanilla extract
- ¼ to ½ teaspoon of salt or to taste

Method

1. Peel and chop the green bananas into 3-4 big pieces each. Blend them with 1/2 cup of milk and water until everything comes together smoothly.
2. Place a pot over medium to high heat and pour in the banana mixture.
3. Add in the nutmeg, cinnamon, salt, and allspice until everything is properly combined.
4. Bring the heat down to low and keep stirring for around 15 minutes or until the porridge has thickened.
5. If required, heat the rest of the milk and pour it slowly to the cooking porridge until you get the desired consistency.

6. Once done, add in the vanilla and condensed milk to sweeten it as per your taste.
7. Enjoy!

Mackerel Rundown

Makes: 3-4 servings

Ingredients

- 16 ounces of pickled or salted mackerel
- ½ of a medium sized onion, sliced
- 3 cups of coconut milk
- ½ of a medium sized tomato, chopped
- 2 cloves of garlic, chopped
- 1 stalk of scallion, chopped
- ½ teaspoon of thyme, dried
- 2 slices of hot pepper

Method

1. Prepare the fish by removing the bones then cutting it into 2 to 3 inch pieces. Place the fish in a bowl that can handle heat and pour in boiling water over it, submerging it completely. Let it soak for around 30 minutes. Once done, drain it out and set the mackerel aside.
2. Place a saucepan over medium to high heat, pour in the coconut milk and bring it to a boil. Keep stirring until the milk reduces down to a thick and custard-like consistency and oil is visible on the surface.
3. At this point, add in the tomato, garlic, hot pepper, thyme, onion, and scallion and stir until everything is combined and coated properly; sauté until the onions turn transparent.

4. Place the fish on the pan making sure the skin side is facing down. Scoop the sauce and cover the top of the fish. Bring the heat down to low.
5. Allow it to simmer for around 10 minutes or until the fish has cooked.
6. Serve with bammies or with boiled dumplings and boiled green bananas.

Steamed Cabbage and Saltfish

Makes: 2 servings

Ingredients

- 4 ounces of saltfish – salted codfish, dried
- ½ of a medium sized cabbage, chopped
- 1 tablespoon of margarine
- 1 sprig of fresh thyme
- ¼ of sweet green pepper, sliced
- 1 clove of garlic, minced (or 1 teaspoon of garlic powder)
- ½ of a medium sized onion, chopped
- Salt to taste
- Black pepper to taste
- 2-3 tablespoons of water
- ½ of hot pepper, with the seeds removed

Method

1. To get rid of the excess salt in the saltfish, soak it in water for a few hours or boil it for 6-8 minutes.
2. Flake the fish apart into smaller chunks.
3. In a frying pan, heat the margarine, and the garlic, onion, thyme, and sweet pepper. Sauté for a couple of minutes.
4. Add the chopped cabbage along with the water. Give it a stir then cover the pan and allow it to cook until the cabbage becomes tender.
5. Add the hot pepper, and season with salt and black pepper. Simmer for another 3-4 minutes.
6. Serve it hot with plantains.

Bammy (Cassava Flatbread)

Makes: 3-4

Ingredients

- 8 ounces of sweet cassava
- ½ can of coconut milk
- A pinch of salt

Method

1. Peel the cassava then grate it. Spread cheesecloth that has been double up and place the grated cassava in it. Wring it out to get rid of as much moisture and juices as possible.
2. Once done, sprinkle a pinch or two of salt over the grated and dry cassava and mix until well incorporated.
3. Divide the cassava into 1-cup or half-cup sized portions and flatten them out to discs that are around ½ inch in thickness.
4. Heat some oil for frying in a pan over medium heat, once it's hot enough; add in the bammies you have shaped. Fry for about 8 minutes on each side.
5. Once done, take them out of the frying pan and place the bammies in a shallow plate or dish. Pour in the coconut milk and let the bammies soak for around 5 minutes.
6. Use a fork to transfer the bammies from the soaking and place them back in the frying pan's hot oil. Fry the bammies over medium heat or until they are light golden in color on each side.
7. Serve with Mackerel Rundown or Ackee and Saltfish.

Johnnycakes (Fried Dumplings)

Makes: 7-8

Ingredients

- 2 cups of all-purpose flour
- 1 tablespoon of baking powder
- 2-3 tablespoons of sugar
- 1/3 teaspoon of kosher salt
- 2 tablespoons of butter, unsalted, diced and chilled
- Canola oil for frying
- ½ cup of milk

Method

1. Add the flour, baking powder, salt, and sugar to a large bowl and mix everything. Add in the chilled and diced butter and rub it into the dry mixture until it forms crumbles that are pea-sized.
2. Add in the milk and stir until it forms a sticky dough.
3. Divide the dough into 7-8 equal portions and shape them into balls.
4. Heat oil for frying in a frying pan over medium to high heat. Once it is hot enough, work in batches and add in half of the shaped balls of dough one by one.
5. Fry them until they puff up and are nice and golden brown in color. This will take about 10-12 minutes.
6. Once done, take them out of the oil, and transfer to a plate lined with paper towels to get rid of the excess oil.
7. Serve with ackee and saltfish or mackerel rundown.
8. Enjoy!

Chapter Two: Main Dishes

Jerk Prawns with Callaloo Rice

Makes: 8 servings

Ingredients

For jerk prawns:

- 1 large onion, minced
- 12 cloves garlic, minced
- 8-10 scotch bonnet chilies or more to taste
- 1 teaspoon ground nutmeg
- ½ teaspoon ground cinnamon
- 4 teaspoons whole pimento
- ½ cup vegetable oil
- ½ cup water
- 2 teaspoons salt
- ½ cup spring onions, chopped
- 2 tablespoons ginger, minced
- 4 teaspoons fresh thyme
- 10 whole cloves
- 2 tablespoons brown sugar
- 6 bay leaves
- ½ cup vinegar
- ½ teaspoon black pepper
- 4 pounds prawns

For coconut Callaloo rice:

- 12 stalks callaloo, discard stems, roughly chop the leaves

- 6 cloves garlic, minced
- 2 whole green scotch bonnet
- 6 tablespoons butter
- Salt to taste
- Pepper to taste
- 8 cups coconut milk
- 6 sprigs thyme
- 4 spring onions, finely chopped
- 2 pounds basmati rice
- Sautéed vegetables to serve

Method

1. To make jerk prawns: Add all the ingredients of jerk prawns except prawns into a food processor or blender and blend until smooth.
2. Place prawns in a bowl. Pour the mixture over it. Coat the prawns well. Let it marinate for a while.
3. Set an outdoor grill or BBQ to preheat over medium heat setting.
4. Meanwhile, make the callaloo rice as follows: Pour coconut milk in a large saucepan.
5. Place the saucepan over medium heat. When it begins to simmer, add callaloo.
6. When it begins to boil, add thyme, bonnet peppers, spring onions, thyme and garlic and mix well. Let it simmer for 10 minutes.
7. Stir in the rice and butter.
8. Lower heat and cover with a lid. Cook until rice is al dente.
9. Brush oil over the grill grates. Place prawns on the preheated grill. Cook for 2-3 minutes. Flip sides and

cook the other side for 2-3 minutes. Baste with the marinade while grilling.

10. Serve rice over individual serving plates. Place prawns over it. Serve with sautéed vegetables of your choice.

Fricassee Chicken, Jamaican Style

Makes: 6-8

Ingredients

- 6-8 pieces chicken

For seasoning:

- 2 teaspoons black pepper powder
- 2 teaspoons Maggie chicken seasoning
- 2 teaspoons paprika
- 2 teaspoons Island jerk seasoning
- 2 teaspoons paprika
- 2 teaspoons salt
- 2 teaspoons Maggie all-purpose
- 2 teaspoons cayenne pepper

Other ingredients:

- 2 stalks scallions, chopped
- 2 tablespoons ketchup
- ½ cup vegetable oil or more if required
- A little water
- 1 hot pepper, sliced
- 2 cloves garlic, crushed
- 2 sprigs thyme, chopped
- 2 tomatoes, sliced
- 2 small onions, sliced

Method

1. Mix together all the seasoning ingredients in a bowl. Sprinkle over the chicken pieces.
2. Place it in a bowl. Add scallions, hot pepper, thyme, tomatoes, garlic, thyme and onions and stir. Cover and set aside for a while for the flavors to set in.
3. Place a Dutch oven or skillet over medium heat. Add oil and allow it to heat.
4. Remove only the chicken pieces from the bowl and add a few pieces at a time and cook until brown.
5. Add the cooked chicken into another skillet. Add the other ingredients that were in the bowl along with the chicken.
6. Add ketchup and water and stir. Place the skillet over medium heat.
7. When it begins to boil, lower heat and cover with a lid. Simmer until the gravy is thickened.
8. Serve over rice or anything of your choice.

Vegan Lentil Patties

Serves: 4

Ingredients

For the filling:

- ½ tablespoon coconut oil
- 1 clove garlic, minced
- ¼ teaspoon dried thyme
- ¼ teaspoon ground cumin
- 1/8 teaspoon ground allspice
- 1/8 teaspoon ground turmeric
- Paprika to taste
- ¼ cup onions, finely chopped
- 1 small spring onion, chopped
- ¼ cup brown lentils, rinsed
- ½ tablespoon tamari or coconut aminos
- Salt to taste
- Cayenne pepper to taste (optional)
- 1 cup water or vegetable broth

For crust:

- 1 cup oat flour
- 2 tablespoons potato starch
- ½ teaspoon baking powder
- 1 teaspoon curry powder
- 2 tablespoons tapioca flour
- ½ tablespoon ground flax seeds
- ¼ teaspoon salt
- ¼ cup almond milk

Method:

1. Place a saucepan over medium high heat. Add oil. When the oil is heated, add onion, garlic and spring onion and sauté until onions are translucent.
2. Add thyme, spices and lentils and stir until the lentils are well coated in the mixture.
3. Pour water and stir. When it begins to boil, lower heat and cover with a lid.
4. Simmer until tender and nearly dry.
5. Add tamari, salt and cayenne pepper and stir.
6. Turn off the heat and cool for a while.
7. To make crust: Add all the dry ingredients into a bowl. Add vegan butter and cut with a pastry cutter or with your hands until crumbly in texture.
8. Add almond milk and mix using your hands and form dough.
9. Divide the dough into 4 equal portions and shape into balls.
10. Place a ball between 2 pieces of parchment paper and roll into a disc of about 4-inch diameter.
11. Place 1 tablespoon of the lentil mixture on one half of the disc. Fold the other half over it, lifting along with the parchment paper. Press with a fork to seal the edges
12. Repeat the above 3 steps with the remaining 3 balls of dough.
13. Bake in a preheated oven at 400° F for 20-25 minutes or until golden brown in color.
14. Serve hot or warm.

Saltfish and Baked Beans

Makes: 6-8 servings

Ingredients

- 1 pound saltfish (cod fish), boneless
- 2 ripe tomatoes, sliced
- 2 cloves garlic, sliced or crushed
- 8 teaspoons vegetable oil
- 2 tablespoons ketchup
- Hot pepper to taste
- 1 onion, sliced
- 2 cans (10 ounces each) baked beans, drained
- Water, as required

Method

10. Soak the saltfish overnight or for about 8 hours by submerging it in cold water in order to remove the excess salt. Throughout this time period, drain out the water and add fresh water a few times.
11. Remove the scales from the saltfish.
12. Add some cold water to a pan and bring it to a boil over high heat. Once it starts boiling, bring the heat down to medium low and add in the saltfish. Allow it to simmer gently for about 20 minutes or until the fish is tender.
13. When done, remove the fish and shred into smaller pieces.
14. Place a Dutch oven or a deep skillet over medium low heat. Add oil. When the oil is heated, add onion,

tomato, garlic and hot pepper and stir-fry until onions are soft.

15. Add saltfish and stir. Cook for a minute.
16. Add rest of the ingredients and stir.
17. Lower heat and cover with a lid. Simmer for 2-3 minutes. Turn off the heat.
18. It can be served right away or cooled for a few minutes and served later.

Honey Glazed Jerk Ham

Makes: 6 servings

Ingredients

- 3 pounds smoked ham leg bone in
- 5-6 cloves
- 1-2 tablespoons smoky jerk marinade

For glaze:

- 2 tablespoons honey
- ½ teaspoon brown sugar
- ½ teaspoon ginger powder
- ½ cup coca –cola
- 1 teaspoon cornstarch mixed in water
- Salt to taste

Method

1. Discard all the packaging material and place ham in a roasting pan. Pour 2-3 cups water all around the ham.
2. Wrap tightly with ham and place it in the oven.
3. Let it cook in a preheated oven at 350° F. The time for cooking is approximately 20-25 minutes per pound of meat.
4. Discard skin and remove excess fat. Score the meat all over with a sharp knife. The cuts should go through the fat as well as a little in the meat.
5. Rub jerk marinade all over. Insert the cloves in the slits.
6. Place it back in the oven for 15 minutes.

7. Meanwhile, place a saucepan with all the glaze ingredients over low heat. Stir until well combined.
8. Remove meat from the oven and brush glaze all over it.
9. Roast for another 10 minutes.
10. Slice and serve.

BBQ Wings

Makes: 4 servings

Ingredients:

- 2 pounds package cut chicken wings
- 1 teaspoon smoky paprika
- Oil, as required, to fry
- 1 tablespoon brown sugar
- ½ cup flour
- 4 tablespoons BBQ sauce or more to taste
- ¼ teaspoon salt or to taste
- Pepper to taste

Method

1. Line 1- 2 baking sheets with parchment paper.
2. Trim the chicken of excess fat. Cut off the tips of each wing. Trim the skin. Dry with paper towels.
3. Add pepper, salt and paprika into a bowl and mix well. Sprinkle this mixture over the wings.
4. Coat the wings in flour.
5. Place a shallow pan over medium heat. Add oil and let it heat. It should be well heated but not smoking.
6. Add wings in batches and fry until crisp.
7. Remove with a slotted spoon and place on a plate lined with paper towels.
8. Place wings in a bowl. Pour BBQ sauce over it. Toss well and serve right away.

Grilled Filet of Beef with Jamaican Rum Glaze

Serves: 2

Ingredients

- 1 tablespoon unsalted butter
- 2 cloves garlic, minced
- 1 shallot, minced
- ½ cup Myer's dark rum
- 1 tablespoon ancho puree
- Salt to taste
- Freshly ground pepper to taste
- 1 ½ cups chicken stock
- 1 tablespoon molasses
- 2 filet mignon steaks (8 ounces each)

Method

1. Place a saucepan over medium high heat. Add butter. When butter melts, add garlic and shallots and sauté until translucent.
2. Add rum and boil until it reduces to 3-4 tablespoons.
3. Stir in the stock. When it begins to boil, lower heat and continue simmering until it reduces to about a cup.
4. Meanwhile, preheat a grill. Sprinkle salt and pepper over the steaks and place on the grill.
5. Grill until the way you like it cooked.
6. Pour the cooked sauce over the steak and serve.

Grilled Pork Jerky with Mango Salsa and Roasted Banana

Makes: 3-4 servings

Ingredients

- 1 ½ pounds pork loin, boneless
- 1 mango, peeled, pitted, finely chopped
- 1 banana, peeled, sliced
- 1 small jalapeño, deseeded, finely chopped
- 1 ½ tablespoons extra-virgin olive oil
- 1 tablespoon lime juice
- 1 ½ tablespoons dry Jamaican jerk seasoning
- 1 small red onion, finely chopped
- ½ cup fresh cilantro, chopped

Method

1. Dry the pork by patting with paper towels. Sprinkle jerk seasoning over the pork and rub it well into it. Place in a bowl. Cover and let it sit for 45-60 minutes.
2. Next rub oil over the pork and place on a baking sheet.
3. Bake in a preheated oven at 350° F for 30-45 minutes. When done, let it sit for 10 minutes.
4. Meanwhile, make salsa as follows: Spread the banana slices on another baking sheet.
5. Bake for 25 minutes or until they begin to get golden brown. Remove the oven and cool.
6. Transfer into a bowl. Add rest of the ingredients and stir.
7. Slice the pork and serve with salsa.

Meat Pie Footballs

Makes: 8 pies

Ingredients

- 1 teaspoon fresh thyme leaves, chopped
- 1 clove garlic, chopped
- 1 small green bell pepper, deseeded, chopped
- 1 teaspoon Jamaican curry powder
- 1 tablespoon vegetable oil
- 1 package (17.3 ounces) puff pastry
- Barbecue sauce or chutney or ranch dressing to serve
- 3 scallions, chopped
- 1 small scotch bonnet chili or habanero, deseeded, chopped
- 4 ounces ground beef
- 1/8 teaspoon ground allspice
- Freshly ground pepper to taste
- Salt to taste
- 1 small egg, beaten with a tablespoon water

Method

1. Add thyme, garlic, bell pepper and scallions into the food processor bowl and pulse until finely chopped.
2. Place a nonstick skillet over medium heat. Add beef and cook until light brown.
3. Add the finely chopped vegetables, allspice and curry powder and cook until beef is brown. Turn off the heat.

4. Add oil, salt and pepper and stir. Taste and adjust the seasoning if necessary. Cool completely.
5. Dust your countertop with a little flour. Place the puff pastry sheets and roll until it is 1/8 inch thick.
6. Use an oval shaped cutter and cut out 4 ovals from each of the pastry sheets. Set aside the scraps.
7. Place 1 tablespoon of the beef mixture on the center of 4 of the ovals. Brush egg on the edges. Cover with the remaining 4 ovals. Seal the edges with a fork.
8. Place the ovals on a baking sheet lined with baking paper.
9. Now cut 8 strips of 2 x 1/8 inch from the dough scrap and 24 strips of 1 x 1/8 inch strip.
10. Place the long strips along the length of the patties and the short strips crosswise in such a manner that it resembles a football.
11. Brush with egg.
12. Bake in a preheated oven at 350° F for 30-45 minutes or until golden brown. When done, let it sit for 10 minutes.
13. Serve meat pie footballs with ranch dressing or barbecue sauce as a dip.

Grilled Lobster Tail with Jerk Sauce and Coconut Rice

Makes: 8-10

Ingredients

For coconut rice:

- 2 tablespoons vegetable oil
- 2 ½ cups coconut milk
- ½ cup fresh cilantro, chopped
- 4 cups basmati rice, rinsed, drained
- 2 teaspoons kosher salt
- 4 scallions, thinly sliced

For jerk sauce:

- 6 tablespoons vegetable oil
- 2 inches piece fresh ginger, peeled, minced
- 8 cloves garlic, minced
- 2 scotch bonnet peppers, halved
- 2 fresh bay leaves
- 2 bunches scallions, chopped, set aside a little for garnishing
- 1 teaspoon ground cinnamon
- 4 teaspoons ground allspice
- 1 teaspoon nutmeg, grated
- Kosher salt to taste
- 1 cup chicken stock
- 6 tablespoons soy sauce
- Juice of 4 limes

- Zest of 2 limes, grated
- ¼ cup fresh thyme, chopped
- ½ cup fresh cilantro, chopped
- 1 cup dark brown sugar

For lobster:

- 2 sticks unsalted butter, at room temperature
- 8 lobster tails (10-12 ounces each), halved lengthwise

Method

1. To make coconut rice: Place a large saucepan (that has a tight fitting lid) over medium heat.
2. Add oil. When the oil is heated, add rice and sauté for a few minutes until opaque.
3. Add coconut milk, 3 cups water, salt and stir. When it begins to boil, simmer until the water is almost the same as the rice.
4. Cover with a tight fitting lid and lower heat to low heat. Let the rice cook for 15 minutes.
5. Stir and cover again. Remove from heat. Using a fork, fluff the rice. Stir in scallions and cilantro.
6. To make jerk sauce: Place a saucepan over medium high heat. Add oil. When the oil is heated, add ginger, garlic, and scallions and scotch bonnet chili and sauté until fragrant.
7. Add all the spices, salt and fresh bay leaf. Sauté for a few seconds until fragrant.
8. Add brown sugar, thyme, stock, soy sauce and zest. Let it cook for 6-7 minutes.
9. Add lime juice and half the cilantro.
10. Set aside half the sauce for dipping.

11. To make lobster: Set a grill to preheat to medium high heat. Coat a little of the remaining sauce on the flesh side of the lobster. Place lobster on the grill, with the flesh side facing down.

12. Grill until golden brown. It should take around 5 minutes. Turn sides and baste again with remaining sauce. Cook until the flesh begins to come away from the shells.

13. Spread coconut rice on a serving platter. Place lobster tails over the rice.

14. Brush lobster tails with a little butter. Drizzle remaining jerk sauce all over the rice and sprinkle cilantro and scallion greens.

Butterflied Leg Lamb with Jamaican Papaya Salsa

Makes: 6 servings

Ingredients

- 3 pounds leg of lamb, boneless, butterflied, halved along the length
- 2 tablespoons dried thyme
- Kosher salt to taste
- ½ tablespoon sherry vinegar
- 1 scallion, sliced
- 1 small red bell pepper, deseeded, chopped
- ¼ cup extra virgin olive oil
- 1 teaspoon ground allspice
- ½ tablespoon dark brown sugar
- ½ teaspoon fresh ginger, peeled, grated
- ½ cup ripe papaya pieces, peeled, deseeded
- 1 small habanero pepper, deseed if desired, minced

Method

1. Set a grill to preheat to medium high heat.
2. Brush half the oil over the lamb. Rub ½ tablespoon thyme on each side of the lamb leg pieces. Also rub ¼ teaspoon allspice and salt liberally on each side of the lamb pieces.
3. Place lamb with the fat side down on the grill. Cook until brown. Flip sides and cook the other side until brown or the internal temperature of meat in the thickest part shows 130 - 135 ° F according to the way you like it cooked.

4. When done, place lamb on your chopping board. Cover lamb with foil, loosely. Let it sit for 10 minutes. Slice the lamb and place on individual serving plates.

5. Meanwhile, add remaining oil, vinegar, brown sugar, ginger and ¼ teaspoon salt into a bowl. Stir until sugar dissolves completely.

6. Stir in scallions, bell pepper, papaya and habanero pepper. Toss well.

7. Sprinkle some salt over the lamb and serve with papaya salsa.

Chicken Curry with Coconut Milk

Makes: 6 servings

Ingredients

For Jamaican curry powder:

- 1 ½ tablespoons cumin seeds
- 1 ½ tablespoons fenugreek seeds
- 1 ½ tablespoons black peppercorns
- 2 teaspoons whole allspice
- 1 ½ tablespoons mustard seeds
- 1 ½ tablespoons anise seeds
- 1 ½ tablespoons coriander seeds
- 1 ½ tablespoons turmeric powder

For chicken curry:

- 4 ½ tablespoons vegetable oil
- Coarse salt to taste
- Freshly ground pepper to taste
- 6 cloves garlic, minced
- 1 medium scotch bonnet pepper, minced
- 3 tablespoons fresh thyme, chopped
- 3 cups coconut milk
- 6 chicken legs, skinless, split
- 3 medium onions, thinly sliced
- 1 ½ tablespoon ginger, minced
- 6 tablespoons Jamaican curry powder or use as per your taste
- 4 ½ cups chicken stock
- Juice of a lime

Method

1. To make Jamaican curry powder: Add cumin, fenugreek, mustard, coriander seeds, black peppercorns and allspice into a skillet.
2. Place the skillet over medium heat. Roast until a sweet aroma is in the air. Turn off the heat. Let it cool completely.
3. Transfer into a spice grinder and grind until fine. Add into a bowl. Add turmeric powder and stir well.
4. To make chicken curry: Sprinkle salt and pepper over the chicken.
5. Place a Dutch oven over high heat. Add oil. When the oil is heated, add chicken and cook until brown. Cook in batches if required. Remove the chicken with a slotted spoon and place on a plate lined with paper towels.
6. Place the pot back over heat. Stir in the onions, chili pepper, garlic and ginger. Sauté for a few minutes until onions are translucent.
7. Stir in thyme and curry powder and sauté for a few seconds until fragrant.
8. Add lime juice and stir. Add the chicken back into the pot. Pour stock and coconut milk.
9. When it begins to boil, lower heat and cover partially. Simmer until the chicken is well cooked and is falling off the bone. It may take 1-1 ½ hours. Remove any fat that may be floating on top.

Pork Stew

Makes: 2-3

Ingredients

- 12 ounces of pork – cut it into 1" sized pieces
- 4 tablespoons of ketchup
- 1 tablespoon of soy sauce
- 4 tablespoons of water
- ½ of 1 19 ounce can of pineapple tidbits – drained (preserve the syrup or juice)
- Pepper to taste
- ½ of sweet green pepper, chopped
- 1 tablespoon of vinegar
- ½ of a medium sized onion, chopped
- ½ tablespoon of oil
- 1 tablespoon of brown sugar
- ½ teaspoon of salt
- 1 tablespoon of cornstarch

Method

1. In a medium-sized saucepan, heat some oil over medium heat and add in the onions and pork.
2. Brown them gently; this will take a few minutes to achieve.
3. Take the cornstarch, sugar, and salt in a mixing bowl and combine. Slowly add in the soy sauce, vinegar, water, ketchup, and the juice or syrup preserved from the pineapple.
4. Add the mixture to the pork and stir. Allow it to cook on a low heat and keep stirring until it is clear and thick in consistency.

5. Cover the saucepan and allow it to simmer for around 1 hour.
6. Once done, add in the green pepper and pineapple tidbits then let it cook for another 5 minutes.
7. Serve with steaming hot rice.

Curry Goat

Makes: for 3-4 people

Ingredients

- 24 ounces of goat meat
- 1 tablespoon of curry powder
- 1 tablespoon of white vinegar
- 1 stalk of scallion, chopped
- ½ medium sized onion, chopped
- ½ teaspoon of ginger, chopped
- 2 cloves of garlic, chopped
- ¼ of hot pepper, chopped
- 1 teaspoon of fresh thyme, chopped
- ½ teaspoon of salt
- ½ teaspoon of black pepper
- 2 cups of water, boiling
- 2 tablespoons of vegetable oil
- ½ of a medium-sized carrot, sliced
- ½ large Irish potato, diced
- 2 allspice berries, whole and crushed

Method

1. Cut the meat into pieces that are bite-sized then wash using a mix of vinegar and water.
2. Place the meat in a bowl; add half a tablespoon of the curry powder, onion, ginger, scallion, thyme, black pepper, hot pepper, salt, and garlic to the meat and rub all of these seasonings properly into the pieces. Cover the bowl and let it marinate for 2 hours.

3. Place a skillet over medium heat, and heat some oil in it. Add in the rest of the curry powder and also the meat you have marinated. Let it sear then carefully turn the pieces of the meat and add the boiling water.

4. Cover the skillet and let it simmer for one hour and twenty minutes or until the meat turns tender.

5. Once that is done, add the potato and let it cook for another 5 minutes.

6. Lastly, fold in the allspice berries and carrot and give it a final cooking of 5 minutes.

7. Serve hot with rice.

Escovitch Fish

Makes: 2-3

Ingredients

- 2-3 whole medium or small sized snappers – or Parrot, Grount, or Goat Fish – Clean and scale, leave the tail and head on
- ¾ teaspoon of pepper
- ¾ teaspoon of salt
- 2 cloves of garlic
- White vinegar
- Cooking oil
- 1 scotch bonnet pepper
- 1 onion
- 5 pimento/allspice seeds

Method

1. Make sure the fish is cleaned and scaled properly. Wash it with water and then give it a wash with a mixture of water and vinegar.
2. Once washed, dry them using paper towels; then place them on a plate and set it aside.
3. On each side of each fish – cut some small but deep gashes.
4. Take the salt and pepper and rub them into these gashes and all over the fish. Then place them back on the plate.
5. Heat some oil in a frying pan to shallow fry the fish – take enough oil to partially submerge the fish. Do not submerge it completely.

6. Add one clove of garlic to the pan and turn the heat to high. After 30 seconds or so, remove the garlic from the pan.

7. Next, place the fish very carefully in the hot. Do not overcrowd the pan, just place as many as can be accommodated by the pan.

8. Fry until it is crisp on one side then turn it to the other side carefully and fry until crisp. Bring the heat down as and when required.

9. Once done, transfer them to a plate that has been lined with paper towels.

10. Take the scotch bonnet pepper and onion – slice both of them.

11. Add the sliced scotch bonnet pepper, pimento, and onions in a small sized pot, add in some vinegar, make sure you add enough to submerge everything else in the pot. Boil everything for around 3-4 minutes. Be careful as it boils – avoid letting it overheat as it could make your eyes burn.

12. Pour the spicy vinegar mix over the fried fish to induce a spicy and hot flavor.

Jerk Chicken

Makes: 3

Ingredients

- 3 chicken breast halves, boneless and cut into bite-sized chunks
- ½ cup of water
- Juice of 2 limes
- ¼ teaspoon of ground nutmeg
- 1 teaspoon of ground allspice
- ½ teaspoon of brown sugar
- ½ teaspoon of salt
- 1 teaspoon of thyme, dried
- ¾ teaspoon of black ground pepper
- 1 onion, chopped
- 1 tablespoon of vegetable oil
- ½ teaspoon of ground ginger
- 3/4cup of green onions, chopped
- 1 habanero pepper, chopped
- 3 cloves of garlic, chopped

Method

1. Cut the chicken into bite-sized chunks and place them in a bowl. Drizzle the lime juice over it and mix it well enough to coat all the chunks in the lime juice. Set it aside.
2. Add the nutmeg, allspice, salt, thyme, brown sugar, black pepper, vegetable oil, and ginger to a food processor and blend. Then add in the chopped green

onions, chopped onion, chopped habanero, and garlic and blend until everything is properly combined and almost smooth.

3. Save a third of the mixture for later use and add the rest to the bowl of chicken. Mix it well and make sure all the chunks of chicken are properly coated in the marinade. Cover the bowl and place it in the refrigerator for around 2 hours, minimum.

4. Once that is done, heat a grill pan with some oil. Place the chicken on it and allow it to cook slowly. Turn the chunks frequently and baste them often using the marinade you have saved. Cook until the chicken has cooked through.

Beef Patties

Makes: 5-6

Ingredients

Piecrust:

- 2 cups of all-purpose flour
- ¼ tablespoon of salt
- 2 ½ ounces of shortening
- 1 tablespoon of sugar
- ¼ teaspoon of turmeric
- ½ tablespoon of cider vinegar
- 2 ½ ounces of butter
- ½ cup of iced water

Beef filling:

- 8 ounces of ground beef
- ½ teaspoon of garlic, granulated
- ¼ of a medium sized onion, chopped
- ½ teaspoon of paprika
- ½ teaspoon of curry powder
- ¼ teaspoon of allspice powder
- ½ teaspoon of white pepper
- ½ thyme, dried
- 1-2 green onions, chopped
- ¼ teaspoon or more or less of salt
- 1 tablespoon of parsley, fresh and chopped
- ¼ teaspoon of chili powder
- 3 tablespoons of breadcrumbs

- ½ teaspoon of chicken bouillon powder
- ¼ scotch bonnet pepper, chopped – optional
- 1 egg white for brushing

Method

1. Add the flour, sugar, salt, and turmeric to a food processor and blend until everything is properly combined. This can also be done by hand.
2. Add in the shortening, vinegar, butter and the water in installments. Keep pulsing until the mixture is properly combined and forms enough into a dough that holds shape like a ball.
3. Lightly flour a working surface and place the dough on it then roll the dough out.
4. Once rolled out, put it in the fridge for about 30 minutes or until it is ready to be used.
5. Using a bowl or glass, cut out as many circles as possible. Once you have cut all of the dough away into circles, refrigerate them for around 30 minutes or until they are ready to be sued.
6. Now, as they rest in the refrigerator, prepare your beef pie filling by placing a saucepan over medium heat and adding a tablespoon of oil. Once it's hot, add in the onions, paprika, garlic, curry powder, thyme, white pepper, allspice, chili powder and the bouillon. Allow it to simmer for around 2 minutes.
7. Once done, add in the ground beef, along with the breadcrumbs and let it cook for around 10 minutes or minutes. Keep stirring it to prevent it from burning. Add ¼ cup of water.
8. Next, add the parsley and green onions, give it a taste and adjust the pepper and salt seasoning.

9. Take it off the heat and allow it to cool.
10. Assembly – once the filling has cooled down completely, scoop out one tablespoon of the beef filling; place it in the middle of each circle of dough. Brush the edges of the circle with some egg white and fold the circle over and twist it, using your fingers, keep twisting around the edges until they are fully closed. Be gentle and properly seal the edges of the meat pie.
11. You can also seal the dough circles by pressing the edges down with a fork.
12. Preheat the oven to 375F.
13. Prepare a baking sheet by lining it with parchment paper.
14. Place the pies carefully on the prepared baking sheet.
15. Bake for 30 minutes.
16. Serve warm. Enjoy!

Steamed Fish

Makes: 4

Ingredients

- 4 red snappers, whole, scaled and cleaned
- 2 teaspoons of fresh thyme, chopped
- 2 whole lemons
- 2 medium-sized onions, sliced
- 2 teaspoons of minced garlic
- 2 teaspoons of paprika
- 1 teaspoon of grated ginger
- 1 teaspoon of allspice
- 2 medium-sized tomatoes, diced
- 4 green onions, chopped
- 2 bell peppers, sliced
- 2 hot peppers, or as per taste
- 4 cups fish stock, or more or less
- 4 or more cups of chopped vegetables – chayote, potatoes, carrots
- 2 teaspoon bouillon powder or cubes – optional
- Salt and pepper to taste
- 4 tablespoons of butter
- Black pepper to taste

Method

1. Clean and scale the fish. Rinse it then drain it carefully and pat it dry using paper towels. Once done, rub it using lemon.
2. Take a large bowl or shallow pan and place the fish in it and season it with ginger, half of the garlic, salt,

black pepper, and half of the thyme. Turn the fish and rub all the seasonings all over to make sure they are coated well.

3. Place the dish in the refrigerator and let it marinate for thirty minutes or even overnight.
4. Add 2 or more tablespoons of oil to a large skillet and heat it. Add in the onion, garlic, thyme, allspice, and paprika.
5. Add in the veggies and add the ones that have the longest cooking time first – like potatoes. Then add in the fish stock and bring everything to a boil. Once it starts boiling, cover it then allow it to simmer for about 5 minutes.
6. Carefully place the fish in the boiling stock and add in the green onion, tomato, and hot pepper.
7. Spoon the stock on top of the fish then cover and allow it to steam over medium heat for around 4-5 minutes or until the meat is tender on each side – cooking time may vary depending on how thick the fish is.
8. Add the butter over the fish before you take it off the stove.
9. Serve with rice or crackers.

Brown Stew Chicken

Makes: 10-12

Ingredients

- 2 small whole chickens, cut down to portions
- 6-8 stalks of scallions, chopped
- 2 large tomatoes
- 2 large onions, chopped
- 2 scotch bonnet peppers, chopped
- 4 cloves of garlic, chopped
- ½ cup of lime juice
- 2 medium-sized carrots, finely chopped
- 5-6 sprigs of fresh thyme or 3-4 teaspoons of dried thyme
- 4 tablespoons of soy sauce
- 1-2 teaspoons of allspice, cracked
- 4 cups of coconut milk, unsweetened
- 2 tablespoons of coconut oil
- 4 teaspoons of cornstarch, or 1 tablespoon of flour

Method

1. Pour the lime juice over the chicken you have cut down to portions. Rub the lime juice all over the chicken and make sure it gets an even coating. Drain out the excess juice.
2. Take a large bowl and combine the scallion, tomatoes, onions, thyme, soy sauce, allspice, pepper, and garlic along with the pieces of chicken. Cover it and let it marinate for around 1 hour.
3. Heat some oil in a large saucepan. As you take the pieces of chicken out of the marinade, shake the

seasonings of each individual piece. Reserve this marinade to be used for sauce.

4. Brown the chicken lightly over high heat, do it a few pieces of chicken at a time. Once a batch is done, place them on a plate.

5. Drain the excess oil off the chicken and place them back in the pan. Add the marinade on top of the chicken followed by the carrots.

6. Give everything a nice stir then allow it to cook on medium heat for around 10 minutes.

7. Mix the coconut milk and flour then pour it into the stew, keep stirring continuously.

8. Bring the heat down to low and then allow it to cook for 20 minutes or until the chicken is tender.

9. Serve hot, and enjoy!

Pork Chops

Makes: 2

Ingredients

- 2 pork loin chops, boneless
- ½ tablespoon of orange juice
- ½ tablespoon of soy sauce
- ½ tablespoon of olive oil
- 1-2 green onions, minced
- 2 cloves of garlic, minced
- ½ teaspoon of allspice, ground
- ¼ teaspoon of salt
- ½ teaspoon of dried thyme
- ¼ teaspoon of ginger
- ¼ teaspoon of pepper
- A pinch of cayenne

Method

1. Prepare the pork chops by slashing off some of the fat around the chops – slash at intervals. This is to remove the excess fat while keeping just enough for it to cook in.
2. Take a bowl and add in the salt, soy sauce, pepper, orange juice and oil. Stir everything up.
3. Add in the garlic, green onion, thyme, allspice, ginger, cayenne, and thyme. Mix well.
4. Take this mixture and rub it on both sides of the chops. Make sure to rub the seasonings and spices in properly. Let it rest for 1 hour to enhance the flavors.
5. Preheat the oven to 375F.

6. Lightly grease a roasting pan. Place the marinated chops in it.
7. Roast and turn the chops halfway through.
8. Roast until the chops have browned and the juices they give off are running clear when you pierce it with a knife or fork. This will take about 20 minutes.
9. Serve hot, and enjoy!

Curry Chicken

Makes: 4

Ingredients

- 24 ounces of chicken
- Onion powder, as per taste
- 2 ounces of curry powder
- 1 teaspoon of salt
- 2 tablespoons of oil
- 1-2 teaspoons of garlic powder
- 1 tablespoon of vinegar
- 1 medium-sized potato, diced
- ¼ to ½ teaspoon of black pepper - optional
- ¼ cup of water
- 1 sprig of thyme – optional

Method

1. Slice the chicken into 4 or more pieces. Wash the chicken with a mixture of water and vinegar.
2. Place the chicken in a bowl and add in all of the ingredients.
3. Rub the spices and seasonings into the chicken thoroughly until the powders are wet and stick to the chicken properly.
4. Place a skillet over high heat and heat the cooking oil along with a tablespoon of curry powder, until the powder changes in color.
5. Add in the pieces of chicken to the skillet and reduce the heat to medium, instantly followed by water.
6. Add in the potato and cover the pot. Allow it to simmer.

7. Give everything in the pot a nice stir and taste to check the salt and seasoning of the gravy.
8. Make whatever adjustments required.
9. Optional – add in the black pepper and thyme.
10. Let it simmer and cook until the chicken is tender.
11. Once done, remove the chicken pieces out of the skillet and into a bowl.
12. Turn the heat to high and allow the gravy to cook a bit to thicken it.
13. Once it has reduced considerably to a desired consistency, turn the heat off, and add the chicken back.
14. Serve hot, and enjoy!

Oxtail with Broad Beans

Makes: 2

Ingredients

- 8 ounces of beef oxtail, cut down to pieces
- 1 green onion, sliced thinly
- 1 -sized onion, chopped
- 1 clove of garlic, minced
- ½ of a scotch bonnet pepper, chopped
- ½ teaspoon of fresh ginger, minced
- 1 tablespoon of soy sauce
- 1 sprig of thyme, fresh and chopped
- ¼ teaspoon of salt
- 1 tablespoon of vegetable oil
- ½ teaspoon of black pepper
- ¾ cup of water
- ½ teaspoon of allspice berries, whole
- ½ cup of fava beans, drained
- 2 tablespoons of water
- ½ tablespoon of cornstarch

Method

1. Take the meat in a medium-sized bowl and add in the green onion, scotch bonnet pepper, garlic, onion, thyme, soy sauce, pepper, and salt.
2. Toss the contents of the bowl until everything is properly combined and evenly coated.
3. Heat a skillet over medium to high heat and add in the vegetable oil. Add the meat mixture to the pan and allow the oxtail to brown.

4. Let it brown all over, it will take around.
5. Put everything in a pressure cooker, and add in ¾ cup of water.
6. Cook in the pressure cooker for around 25 minutes.
7. Once done, remove the pressure cooker from the heat, and then very carefully take the lid off.
8. Add in the beans along with the allspice berries and let it come to a simmer on medium to high heat.
9. Mix the cornstarch with the 2 tablespoons of water and add it to the simmering contents, and keep stirring.
10. Stir and cook for a few minutes more until the sauce thickens up and the beans become tender.
11. Serve hot, and enjoy!

Chapter Three: Side Dishes

Boiled Dumplings

Makes:

Ingredients

- 1 ¾ cups all-purpose flour
- Water, as required
- ½ teaspoon salt
- 3-4 inches pumpkin, cubed (do not peel or deseed)
- 1 medium sweet potato, peeled, cubed
- 1 medium yam, peeled, cubed
- 2 inches green banana, peeled, cubed

Method

1. Add flour and ¼ teaspoon salt into a bowl. Add water, a little at a time and mix until dough is formed. If the dough is sticky, add some more flour and knead again.
2. Cover with a clean kitchen towel and set aside.
3. Place a pot over medium high heat. Half fill with water and add about ½ teaspoon salt.
4. Add yam, sweet potato, pumpkin and banana into the pot. Make small discs of the dough and make a dent in the center (like donuts) and add into the pot. Add one dumpling at a time so that they do not stick to each other.
5. Turn off the heat. Remove vegetables and dumplings with a slotted spoon and add into a bowl.
6. Serve with a meat of your choice.

Jamaican Carrots

Makes: 6-7 servings

Ingredients

- 2 pounds carrots, peeled, sliced
- 4 tablespoons brown sugar
- 2 teaspoons fresh lemon juice
- 2 teaspoons ground cumin
- ½ - 1 teaspoon chili powder or to taste
- 2 tablespoons butter
- 2 teaspoons hot sauce
- 2 teaspoons orange juice or pineapple juice
- 4 cloves garlic, peeled, minced
- Salt to taste

Method

1. Place carrots in a saucepan. Pour enough water so that the carrots are covered with water.
2. Place saucepan over medium high heat. Stir occasionally until the carrots are tender. Drain the carrots and add into a bowl.
3. Place the saucepan back over heat. Add butter. When butter melts, add brown sugar, lemon juice, hot pepper sauce, garlic, orange juice, chili powder and cumin powder. Cook for a couple of minutes until aromatic.
4. Add carrots and stir until well coated. Add salt and stir.
5. Serve hot.

Spicy Beans

Makes: 6 servings

Ingredients

- 1 ½ cups dried kidney or other red beans, rinsed, soaked in water overnight, drained, rinsed or 3 cans (15.5 ounces each) drained, rinsed
- 4 ½ cups water
- 1 ½ cups onions, coarsely chopped
- 8 cloves garlic sliced
- 1 ½ cups light coconut milk
- ¾ teaspoon fine sea salt or to taste
- 1 tablespoon kelp flakes (to be used if using dried beans)
- 3 tablespoons extra-virgin olive oil
- 1 ½ cups scallions, keep the white and green parts separate
- ½ teaspoon chipotle chili or red pepper flakes or to taste
- ½ teaspoon ground allspice
- ¾ cup fresh cilantro, chopped

Method

1. If using dried beans, add beans, kelp and water into a pot. Place the pot over high heat. When the water begins to boil, lower heat and cover with a lid. Simmer until beans are tender.
2. Place a large skillet over medium heat. Add oil. When the oil is heated, add onion and sauté until brown.

3. Stir in garlic, scallions and pepper flakes. Cook for a couple of minutes until the scallion greens are bright green color.
4. Add beans, allspice, salt and coconut milk and mix well. Taste and add more seasonings if necessary.
5. Let it simmer until slightly thick. Sprinkle cilantro on top and serve.

Pickled Cucumber

Makes: 4-6 servings

Ingredients

- 2 cucumbers, peeled, thinly sliced
- Juice of 1-2 limes
- ¼ scotch bonnet pepper, finely minced
- 1 small onion, finely minced
- ¾ teaspoon salt
- A handful parsley, chopped

Method

1. Add all the ingredients into a glass bowl. Cover and set aside for a few hours for the flavors to set in.

Fried Mango

Makes: 8

Ingredients

- 1 cup corn meal
- 4 cups flour
- 2 tablespoons baking powder
- 2 firm, ripe mangoes, peeled, pitted, chopped
- 4 tablespoons sugar
- A large pinch salt
- Oil, to fry

Method

1. Add mangoes into a blender. Add a little water and blend until smooth.
2. Add rest of the ingredients except oil into a bowl and stir. Add blended mango and stir.
3. Knead into a dough. Cover with a clean, moist cloth and let it sit for an hour.
4. Make dumplings of sausage shape.
5. Pour 1-2 cups oil in a deep pan. Place pan over medium heat. Let the oil heat. It should not smoke but well heated.
6. Add dumplings and fry until golden brown. Fry in batches.

Easy Corn Pie Recipe

Makes: 3-4

Ingredients

- ½ tablespoon cooking oil
- 1 clove garlic, peeled, minced
- 6 ounces canned corn kernels, drained
- A handful fresh parsley, chopped
- ½ teaspoon salt or to taste
- 6 tablespoons cornmeal
- 2 tablespoons minced onions
- ½ cup carrot, grated
- 7 ounces canned creamed corn
- ½ cup evaporated milk or whole milk
- ¼ teaspoon pepper powder
- ¾ cup cheddar cheese, grated

Method

1. Place a skillet over medium heat. Add oil. When the oil is heated, add onion, garlic and carrots and sauté until onions are soft.
2. Add both the types of corn, salt and pepper. Let it cook for a couple of minutes.
3. Lower heat and add milk and ½ cup cheese. Mix well.
4. Add corn meal, stirring constantly. Keep stirring until the mixture pulls away from the sides of the pan. A way to check is to insert a spoon in the mixture. If the mixture is ready, it will stand for a few seconds and then falls off.

5. Transfer into a baking dish that is sprayed with cooking spray. Top with remaining cheese.
6. Place rack in the center of the oven.
7. Bake in a preheated oven at 350° F for 30 minutes or until cheese melts and golden brown in color. When done, remove from the oven and let it sit for 10 minutes.

Caribbean-Spiced Sweet Potatoes

Makes: 6 servings

Ingredients

- 1 ½ pounds sweet potatoes, peeled, chopped into 1 inch chunks
- ½ teaspoon ground cinnamon
- ¼ teaspoon salt or to taste
- 1 ½ tablespoons coconut oil or vegetable oil
- ½ teaspoon ground ginger
- 1 teaspoon hot pepper sauce or cayenne pepper to taste

Method

1. Add potatoes into a bowl. Drizzle oil over it. Toss well and rub the oil into the potatoes using your hands.
2. Spread on to a nonstick baking sheet.
3. Bake in a preheated oven at 400° F for about 30-40 minutes or until cooked through. Shake the sweet potatoes half way through baking.

Easy Cheesy Macaroni and Cheese

Makes: 2-3 servings

Ingredients

- 6 ounces elbow macaroni
- 1 ½ tablespoons all-purpose flour
- 1 teaspoon mustard
- 1 ¼ teaspoons salt
- ¾ cup extra old cheddar cheese, grated
- ¼ cup parmesan cheese, grated
- ¼ cup mozzarella cheese, grated
- 1 tablespoon melted butter
- 2 tablespoons plain bread crumbs or with Italian seasoning
- 1 tablespoon butter
- 1 ¼ cups milk
- 1/8 teaspoon ground nutmeg
- ¼ teaspoon pepper powder

Method

1. Cook pasta following the instructions on the package but drain the water just before al dente. Rinse under cold running water and place it aside.
2. Place a saucepan over medium heat. Add butter. When butter melts, add flour and sauté for a minute or so until it mildly changes its color.
3. Add milk, stirring constantly until thick.
4. Lower heat to medium low and add mustard, pepper, nutmeg and salt. Remove from heat.

5. Add cheddar cheese, 2 tablespoons Parmesan cheese and mozzarella cheese and mix well.
6. Add pasta and fold gently. Transfer into a baking dish that is greased with a little oil or butter.
7. Add melted butter and breadcrumbs into a bowl and stir. Cool for a while. Add 2 tablespoons Parmesan and mix well. Sprinkle over the pasta.
8. Bake in a preheated oven at 350° F for about 20 minutes or until the top is golden brown.

Callaloo

Makes: 8

Ingredients

- 48 ounces of Callaloo kale and collard greens, fresh
- 6 cloves of garlic, minced
- 4 strips of bacon cut into pieces
- 2 medium-sized onions
- 2 sprigs of fresh thyme
- 1 teaspoon of smoked paprika
- 2 fresh tomatoes
- Salt and pepper to taste
- 2 hot peppers
- 6 plantains, ripe
- Oil for cooking

Method

1. Cut the soft stems and leaves from the branches of Callaloo. Place them in a bowl and add in cold water. Allow to soak for 5 to 10 minutes or until you are done with the prep.
2. Dice the tomatoes, slice the onions, and mince the garlic then set them aside.
3. Take the Callaloo out of the cold water and cut it into chunks.
4. Heat a saucepan and place the bacon. Cook the strips until they are crisp. Once they crisp up, add in the garlic, thyme, and onions, and stir for a minute or so.
5. Next, add in the diced tomatoes, smoked paprika, and hot pepper. Sauté for around 2-3 minutes.
6. Lastly, add the Callaloo along with salt and mix until everything is properly combined and let it steam for around 6 to 8 minutes or until the leaves turn tender.

You can add a small amount of water as required. Give it a taste and adjust whatever seasonings require adjustments then turn the heat off.

7. Take a sharp knife and slice off both the ends of the plantains. Remove the peel by carefully pulling the peel back.

8. Slice them lengthwise and into medium sized pieces and set them aside.

9. Take a large frying pan and grease it with oil, place it on medium heat. Drizzle some oil over the plantain pieces and season with ground pepper and salt.

10. Fry them over medium heat and cook them evenly, tossing them around for an even cooking. Fry until they attain the texture and color desired. Add more salt or pepper if required.

11. Remove from the pan and serve with the Callaloo.

Stew Peas

Makes: 7-8

Ingredients

Stew:

- 3 cup red peas (red kidney beans)
- 24 ounces of stew beef
- 12 ounces of salt beef
- 1 scotch bonnet pepper
- 5 sprigs of thyme
- 3 stalks of scallion
- 3 cup of coconut milk
- 6 cloves of garlic
- 6-7 allspice seeds
- Salt and pepper to taste
- ½ cup water combined with 4 ½ tablespoons of flour for thickening

Spinners:

- 2 cups of all-purpose flour
- Sufficient water to knead with
- ½ to ¾ teaspoon of salt

Method

Spinners:

1. Mix the salt and flour in a bowl. Add half-cup water and mix. Keep kneading and add more water in very little quantities. Form a stiff dough.
2. Roll the dough into pieces that are about an inch long. Place all the shaped spinners spread out in a large plate to prevent them from sticking together. Sprinkle

half a teaspoon of flour over the spinner and toss them to prevent from sticking. Do not add more than half a teaspoon.

Stew:

1. Take the salt beef and boil then drain it. Do this at least twice.
2. Using the same pan, add in the peas, garlic, and meat together in it and boil until the peas become tender. It will take about 90 minutes to achieve.
3. Add in the seasonings, coconut milk, and the shaped spinners. Let it cook for 1 hour.
4. Season with salt and pepper as per your taste preferences.
5. Mix the ½ cup flour with 4 ½ tablespoons of flour and strain it into the pan.
6. Boil the stew until it thickens. Once done, serve it with rice.

Rice and Peas

Makes: 4

Ingredients

- 4 ounces of red kidney beans
- 1 cup and 2 tablespoons of long grain rice, uncooked
- 8 ounces of chicken/vegetable broth or stock
- 16 fl. ounces of water
- ¼ cup of coconut cream
- ¼ teaspoon of allspice, ground
- 1 teaspoon of thyme leaves, fresh
- 1 scallion, chopped finely
- 2 cloves of garlic, minced
- ¼ cup of white onion, chopped
- ½ teaspoon of black pepper
- ½ of a scotch bonnet pepper, seeds removed
- ¾ teaspoon of kosher salt
- ½ teaspoon of brown sugar

Method

1. Rinse the kidney beans and place them in a stockpot. Fill it with water, covering the beans with a few inches of water and let them soak overnight.
2. Drain the beans and rinse them properly.
3. Add the chicken (or vegetable) stock, coconut cream, water, and beans to a saucepan and bring it to a boil.
4. Cover the saucepan, bring the heat down, and allow it to simmer for 45-90 minutes or until the beans become creamy and tender.

5. Add in the allspice, thyme, scallion, garlic, onion, brown sugar, salt, black pepper, scotch bonnet pepper, and the uncooked rice.
6. Make sure the level of the liquid is at least an inch over the rice, and in case it is not – add some more of broth or water to cover it to the desired level.
7. Bring it to a boil, bring the heat down, cover the saucepan and let it simmer for around 20 to 30 minutes or until the rice becomes tender and has cooked through.
8. Serve hot. Enjoy!

Fried Plantain

Makes: 6-8 servings

Ingredients

- 2 plantains, ripe
- 1 ½ tablespoons of nutmeg or cinnamon
- Oil for frying

Method

1. Cut off the ends of the plantains. Make 2 incisions, on opposing sides and lengthwise, of the plantain skin.
2. Peel the skin off.
3. Cut the plantains in half. By width.
4. Slice each half into ¼" thick pieces, slice them long ways.
5. Heat a skillet with oil for frying, on medium heat. The level of oil should be enough to cover the slices.
6. Fry the slices of plantain until they are golden brown in color on both the sides. Each piece would require around 45 seconds or 1 minute for cooking through. Avoid burning or browning it too much.
7. Once they are done, take them out of the skillet using a slotted spoon and place them on a plate that has been layered with paper towels to remove the excess oil.
8. Take the nutmeg or cinnamon and sprinkle it generously, or as per your taste preferences, over the fried plantains.
9. Serve hot or warm. Enjoy!

Steamed Cabbage

Makes: 3

Ingredients

- ½ of a large cabbage
- 1 small carrot
- 1 small onion
- ½ cup of chopped bell peppers – yellow and red
- 2 cloves of garlic
- 1 tablespoon of olive oil
- 1 sprig of thyme
- A dash of black pepper or as per taste
- ¼ of scotch bonnet pepper – optional

Method

1. Cut the ½ cabbage in half. Remove the center and wash the leaves of the cabbage.
2. Slice the leave into smaller pieces and set them aside.
3. Prepare the carrot by peeling, washing, and chopping it into strips – make sure the strips are pretty thin.
4. Chop a third of a red bell pepper and a third of a yellow bell pepper, to get half cup of chopped bell peppers in total.
5. Chop the small onion.
6. Mince the garlic finely.
7. Place a saucepan on medium heat and add in the oil, garlic, thyme, and onion. Keep stirring and cook for around 3 minutes or until the onion softens up a little.
8. Add in the bell pepper, cabbage, scotch bonnet pepper, and carrot. Add salt as per your taste. Stir

everything well until all the ingredients are properly combined.

9. Bring the heat down to low and cover the saucepan. Allow the vegetable to steam until they are tender and soft. Or you could cook them until you get the desired texture, as some people prefer their veggies a little crunchy.

10. Add in the black pepper.

11. Cook for another 2-3 minutes then take it off the heat.

12. Serve hot. Enjoy!

Seasoned Rice

Makes: 2-3

Ingredients

- 4 ounces of salted codfish
- 4 ounces of bacon, chopped
- 1 tablespoon of cooking oil
- 1 small onion, chopped
- 3 tablespoons of chopped red bell pepper
- 3 tablespoons of chopped green bell pepper
- 1 cup of cabbage, chopped
- 1 small tomato, chopped
- 1 cup of butternut squash or Jamaican squash, cut into small chunks
- 1 cup of hot water
- 2 teaspoons of ketchup
- ½ teaspoon of hot pepper sauce
- Salt to taste
- Black pepper to taste
- 1 cup of basmati or long grain rice

Method

1. Soak the salted codfish in cold water for 4-5 hours in order to remove the excess salt.
2. Drain it out and cut or break the fish into smaller pieces. Set it aside until ready for use.
3. Take a saucepan and heat some oil in it. Add in the chopped bacon and fry until it's slightly crispy. Take it out of the pan and set it aside.
4. Add in the tomato, bell peppers, and onion. Stir-fry for a minute.

5. Add in the cabbage and pumpkin, and stir everything. Add in the hot water, salted cod, bacon, ketchup and hot pepper sauce. Give everything a nice stir and check the taste. Add salt and black pepper accordingly. Stir everything again until the seasonings are properly combined. Check the taste again and make the required adjustments.
6. Add the rice and give it a gentle stir. Bring the contents of the saucepan to a boil.
7. Once it starts boiling, bring the heat down to low and cover the saucepan.
8. Allow it to steam and cook until the rice is cooked through. Add some more water depending on what kind of rice has been used.
9. Once the rice is cooked, fluff it up with a fork and serve hot.
10. Enjoy!

Pepperpot stew

Makes: 2

Method

- 11 ounces of stew beef, cut down to large sized chunks
- 2 cloves of garlic
- 1 onion, peel and slice thickly
- 1" of ginger, peel and slice like matchsticks
- ½ teaspoon of cinnamon
- 1 bay leaf
- 2 cloves
- 2 cups of beef stock
- 1 tablespoon of oil
- ½ of a scotch bonnet pepper – remove the seeds and slice
- 1 large floury potato – peel and cut down to chunks
- 1 sweet potato, peel and cut down to chunks
- 7 ounces of butternut squash
- 1 large sprig of thyme
- ¼ cup of coconut milk
- 7 ounces of spinach leaves
- Salt to taste
- Pepper to taste

Method

1. Heat the oil in a casserole and add in the beef, garlic, onion, ginger, stock, and spices.
2. Bring everything to a boil.
3. Bring the heat down to low, cover the casserole and let it simmer gently for around 45 minutes.
4. Once that is done, add in the squash followed by the potato along with the thyme and coconut milk.
5. Bing everything to a boil.

6. Once it starts boiling, bring the heat down again tot low, cover the casserole and allow it to gently simmer for 30 to 45 minutes or until the meat is really tender and the veggies are soft.
7. Add in the spinach leaves and seasonings. Adjust the salt and pepper as per your taste preferences.
8. Cook for another 5 minutes or until the spinach leaves have wilted.
9. Ladle into bowl and serve with crusty bread.
10. Enjoy!

Chapter Four: Soups

Jamaican Chicken and Pumpkin Soup

Makes: 3 servings

Ingredients

- 1 ½ pounds chicken thighs, cut into chunks
- 1 teaspoon garlic minced
- ½ scotch bonnet pepper, chopped
- 1 bay leaf
- 1-2 green onions, chopped
- ½ chayote, cut into chunks
- 1-2 cups butternut squash chunks
- A handful fresh parsley, chopped (optional)
- Salt to taste
- Pepper to taste
- 1 small onion, chopped
- 1 teaspoon fresh thyme, chopped
- ½ teaspoon smoked paprika
- 2 ½-3 cups broth or water
- ½ teaspoon ground allspice
- ½ plantain, peeled, chopped into chunks
- 1 carrot, chopped into chunks
- ½ Grace flavored packet cock soup

Method

1. Place a Dutch oven or soup pot over medium heat. Add oil. When the oil is heated, add onions and garlic and sauté for a couple of minutes.

2. Add green onions, thyme, bay leaf, and allspice and scotch bonnet pepper and cook for a couple of minutes.
3. Stir in the chicken, salt and pepper. Cook for a minute.
4. Add broth and all the vegetables.
5. When it begins to boil, lower heat and cover with a lid. Simmer until the vegetables are tender.
6. Ladle into soup bowls. Serve bread on the side.

Cream of Callaloo Soup

Makes: 4 servings

Ingredients

- 2 cups callaloo, chopped
- ½ teaspoon cayenne pepper
- ½ teaspoon thyme leaves or 1 teaspoon dried thyme
- ¼ cup butter
- 2 cups broth
- ¼ pound medium shrimp, peeled, deveined
- 1 tablespoon cooking oil
- 1 clove garlic, minced
- 2 cups milk
- 6 tablespoons all-purpose flour
- Salt to taste

Method

1. Place a skillet over medium heat. Add oil. When the oil is heated, add onion, garlic and thyme and sauté until onions are translucent.
2. Stir in callaloo, cayenne pepper and salt and cook until it wilts. Turn off the heat.
3. Place a saucepan over low heat. Add butter. When butter melts, add flour and stir constantly until the mixture begins to bubble.
4. Add milk, stirring constantly until thick.
5. Add broth and callaloo mixture and stir.
6. When it begins to boil, lower heat and cover with a lid. Add shrimp now if using.
7. Ladle into soup bowls and serve

Jamaican Mannish Water (Goat Soup)

Makes: 2 servings

Ingredients

- 1 pound goat head and feet, cut into small pieces
- 1 carrot, peeled, diced
- 2-3 grains allspice
- 2 cloves garlic, crushed
- ½ cup flour
- 2 fingers green banana, sliced, do not peel
- ½ green hot pepper, chopped
- ¼ pound pumpkin, chopped
- 1 small Irish potato, cubed
- Salt to taste
- ½ pound yellow yam
- 2 stalks scallions, chopped
- Water, as required

Method

1. Add flour and a pinch of salt into a bowl. Add water, a little at a time and mix until dough is formed. If the dough is sticky, add some more flour and knead again. Cover and set aside for a while.
2. Place a pot half filled with water over high heat. Bring to a boil. Add goat pieces and cook for 10-15 minutes. Turn off the heat. Drain the water.
3. Add goat back into the pot. Add 2 cups water and place the pot over high heat. Add allspice and garlic.

4. Cook until slightly tender. Pour more water if required.
5. Stir in the pumpkin, banana and carrot and simmer for about 10 minutes. Add yam and cook for another 10 minutes.
6. Make small discs and make a dent in the center (like donuts) and add into the pot. Add one dumpling at a time so that they do not stick to each other.
7. Also add thyme, scallion, and salt, pepper hot and pepper. Simmer until the soup thickens.
8. Ladle into soup bowls and serve

Fish Tea

Makes: 2 servings

Ingredients

- 2 small or 1 medium-sized whole fish
- 1 ½ green unripe bananas, sliced
- 4 cups of water
- 1 chayote, sliced
- 1 small onion, sliced
- ½ of a large or 1 small carrot, sliced
- ¼ of green bell pepper, sliced
- ¼ of red bell pepper, sliced
- Salt to taste
- 1 stalk of scallion
- Black pepper to taste
- 1/5 teaspoon of hot pepper sauce
- 2 sprigs of thyme, fresh
- ½ tablespoon of butter
- ½ of a hot pepper

Method

1. Remove the heads of the fish and set them aside. Fillet the fish carefully and set aside the flesh.
2. In a stockpot, place the bones and heads of the fish and add in 2 cups of water and bring everything to a boil.
3. Add in the chayote, carrot, and green bananas to the fish stock and bring it to a quick boil.
4. Add in the bell peppers, scallion, and onion. Add the black pepper and salt as per taste, hot pepper sauce,

and the fresh thyme. Stir everything until properly combined.

5. Place the fillets of fish and the hot pepper over the soup and allow it to simmer over medium to high heat for around 10 minutes.

6. Once that is done, add in the butter, stir it and let it simmer for around 5 minutes.

7. Serve hot. Enjoy!

Chicken Soup

Makes: 3

Ingredients

- 24 ounces of chicken thighs – cut them into bite-sized chunks
- 1 teaspoon of garlic, minced
- ½ of a medium sized onion, diced
- 1 teaspoon thyme, fresh
- ½ teaspoon of smoked paprika
- ½ of a scotch bonnet pepper
- 1 bay leaf
- 1-2 green onions, diced
- 2 ½ or more cups of broth or water
- ½ of a chayote cut into large-sized chunks
- ½ teaspoon of allspice
- ½ of a plantain, cut into chunks
- 1 carrot, cut into large chunks
- 1 ½ cup of butter squash – cut into large chunks
- 1-2 tablespoon of parsley, fresh and chopped
- Salt and pepper to taste
- ½ of a packet of Grace Cock Flavored Soup Mix

Method

1. Heat a Dutch oven or a pot with oil. Add in the green onions, onions, garlic, bay leaf, thyme, allspice, and scotch bonnet pepper to the pot. Stir for around 3 minutes to make sure the aromas have been activated. Add in the chicken, pepper, and salt. Stir for around a minute.

2. Next, pour in the broth or water.
3. Add in the vegetables – squash, plantains, chayote, carrots, and the soup mix.
4. Add the salt as per your taste.
5. Cover the pot and allow it to cook for around 30 minutes.
6. Once done, serve hot with some bread.

Pumpkin Soup

Makes: 2-3

Ingredients

- 1 tablespoon of coconut oil
- 2 cloves of garlic, minced
- ½ cup of onion, minced
- 3 tablespoons of celery, diced
- ½ tablespoon of parsley, fresh and minced
- 1 green onion, chopped – plus extra to garnish with
- 2 cups of Jamaican pumpkin, peel – removed the seeds – cut down to chunks
- 1/5 teaspoon of dried thyme
- ½ cup of carrot, diced
- ½ cup of potato, diced
- ¼ cup of coconut milk, plus more to garnish with
- 2 cups of vegetable stock – you can also use water
- Allspice, just a pinch – optional
- 1/5 teaspoon of cayenne pepper
- Sea salt to taste

Method

1. Take a pot and heat the oil in it. Add in the garlic and onion then sauté for around 3-4 minutes or until the onion softens up.
2. Add in the carrot and celery, and let it cook for 3 minutes or until the celery softens up.
3. Add in the parsley, pumpkin, thyme, stock, pepper, coconut milk, allspice, potato, and green onion.
4. Bring everything to a boil.

5. Once it starts boiling, reduce the heat and allow it to simmer. Cook for around 30 minutes.
6. Once done, let it cool down for a bit, then using a blender, puree everything in batches.
7. Give it a taste to check for the salt. Make the required adjustments.
8. Ladle the soup into bowls and garnish it with coconut milk and some spring onion.
9. Enjoy!

Gungo Peas Soup

Makes: 3

Ingredients

- 1 ½ cup or 1 14 ounce can of gungo peas (pigeon peas) – frozen or fresh
- ½ cup of coconut milk
- 4 cups of water
- 1 small onion, chopped
- 3 tablespoons of red bell pepper, chopped
- 1 green onion, chopped
- ½ of a potato cut into cubes
- 2 cloves of garlic
- ½ of a carrot, chopped
- (Optional) ½ cup of yellow yam – chopped
- 1 sprig of fresh thyme or 1/2 teaspoon of dried thyme
- (Optional) 3-4 allspice/pimento berries
- (Optional) ½ of a scotch bonnet pepper
- Spinners
- Salt to Taste

Spinners:

- 1 cup all-purpose flour
- ¼ teaspoon of salt
- Enough water for binding

Method

Spinners:

1. Mix the salt and flour in a bowl. Add ¼ cup water and mix. Keep kneading and add more water in very little quantities. Form a stiff dough.
2. Roll the dough into pieces that are about an inch long. Place all the shaped spinners spread out in a large plate to prevent them from sticking together. Sprinkle half a teaspoon of flour over the spinner and toss them to prevent from sticking. Do not add more than half a teaspoon.

Soup:

1. Wash and rinse the gungo peas properly.
2. Place them in a pot and add the water. Bring it to a boil.
3. Once it starts boiling, bring the heat down to a simmer and allow it to cook for around 45 minutes or until the peas are tender.
4. Add in the coconut and stir.
5. Add in the rest of the ingredients one by one, along with the shaped spinners. Again, bring it to a boil.
6. Once it starts boiling, bring the heat down and simmer for around 20 minutes.
7. Check the taste and season the soup with salt. Make whatever adjustments are required.
8. Serve hot, and enjoy!

Chapter Five: Dessert

Jamaican Cake

Makes: 10-12

Ingredients

- 1 ½ cups white sugar
- 1 cup + 2 tablespoons pecans, chopped
- 1 ½ bananas, peeled, chopped
- 15 ounces canned, crushed pineapple with its juice
- ¾ teaspoon salt
- 1 cup + 2 tablespoons vegetable oil
- 2 ¼ cups all-purpose flour
- 2 eggs
- 1 ½ teaspoons vanilla extract
- ¾ teaspoon baking soda

Method

1. Add sugar, pecans, oil, bananas and flour into a bowl. Stir well. Make sure that the bananas are not mashed.
2. Pour into a greased cake pan.
3. Bake in a preheated oven at 350° F for about 40-50 minutes or until a toothpick, when inserted in the center, comes out clean.
4. Cool completely. Cut into slices and serve.

Jamaican Coconut Toto

Makes:

Ingredients

- 2 tablespoons butter
- ½ cup sugar
- ½ teaspoon vanilla extract
- ½ teaspoon ground cinnamon
- 1/8 teaspoon nutmeg, grated
- ½ cup evaporated milk
- 1 ½ cups flour
- 1 egg
- 1 ½ tablespoons baking powder
- ½ teaspoon salt
- 1 cup grated coconut

Method

1. Add sugar and butter into a mixing bowl. Beat with an electric mixer until creamy.
2. Add egg and beat again. Add vanilla and beat until well combined.
3. Add flour, cinnamon, baking powder and nutmeg into a bowl and stir.
4. Add flour mixture into the bowl of butter, a little at a time, alternating with a little evaporated milk. Mix until well combined each time.

5. Grease a small shallow baking dish with cooking spray. Pour batter into it.
6. Bake in a preheated oven at 400° F for about 20-30 minutes.
7. Serve it either hot or warm.

Mango Cheesecake

Makes:

Ingredients:

- 2 cups graham cracker crumbs
- 2 teaspoons Jamaican cinnamon powder
- 1 teaspoon salt
- 5 cups Jamaican mango puree
- 4 tablespoons brown sugar
- 6 eggs
- Jest of an orange, grated
- 2 cups sugar
- 1 cup melted butter
- ½ cup peanuts, chopped
- 4 cups sour cream
- 4 teaspoons vanilla extract
- 6 packages cream cheese, softened

Method:

1. Add sour cream, eggs, cream cheese, vanilla, salt, orange zest and mango puree into a bowl and beat with an electric mixer until well combined.
2. Add rest of the ingredients into a bowl and mix well. Transfer into a spring form pan and press it well onto the bottom of the pan.
3. Pour the mango mixture over the crust.
4. Place a roasting pan with the baking pan in an oven. Pour enough water in the roasting pan to cover at least an inch from the bottom of the pan.
5. Bake in a preheated oven at 350° F for about 2 hours.

6. Increase the temperature to 400° F and bake for about 20 minutes.

Sweet Potato Pudding

Makes: 6 servings

Ingredients

- 1 pound sweet potato, grated
- ¼ cup flour
- ½ teaspoon baking powder
- 2 ½ cups coconut milk
- 1 teaspoon vanilla extract
- ¼ teaspoon salt
- 2 tablespoons rum
- 2 ounces yam, grated
- 2 ounces raisins
- 3 ounces evaporated milk
- ½ cup brown sugar
- ¼ teaspoon ground nutmeg
- 2 tablespoons sherry wine
- ½ ounce butter, melted

Method

1. Add potato, yam, baking powder, raisins and flour into a bowl and stir.
2. Add rest of the ingredients into a bowl and whisk well. Pour into the bowl of potatoes and beat until well combined.
3. Grease a small pan with a little oil. Spoon the mixture into the pan. Let it sit for 30 minutes.
4. Bake in a preheated oven at 350° F for about 1-1 ½ hours or until the center is firm.
5. Serve   warm   or   cold.

Grater Cake

Makes:

Ingredients

- 4 cups grated coconut, white parts only
- 1 cup water
- Red or pink food coloring, as required
- 6 cups granulated sugar
- 1 teaspoon peppermint essence

Method

1. Add coconut, sugar and water into a heavy bottomed saucepan.
2. Place the saucepan over medium heat.
3. Cook until soft and sticky. Stir in peppermint essence. Stir constantly for a minute.
4. Drop spoonfuls of the mixture on a greased tray or sheet. Cool completely and serve.

Plantain Tart

Makes:

Ingredients

- 1 pound flour
- 1 teaspoon salt
- 7 ounces shortening
- Ice water, as required

For filling:

- 4 very ripe bananas, peeled, crushed
- 2 tablespoons margarine
- 2 teaspoons vanilla extract
- 1 cup sugar
- 1 teaspoon nutmeg, ground

Method

1. Add flour and salt into a mixing bowl and stir.
2. Add shortening and cut with a pastry cutter. Add flour and mix well until crumbly in texture.
3. Add cold water and mix to form a dough. Cover and set aside for a while.
4. Meanwhile, make the filling follows: Add all the ingredients of the filling into a saucepan. Place the saucepan over low heat. Cook for 3-4 minutes. Turn off the heat.
5. Dust your countertop with a little flour. Place the dough on the countertop. Place the dough on it. Roll with a rolling pin until 1/8 inch thick.

6. Cut into round shapes.
7. Place a little of the filling on one half of the round. Fold the other half over the filling. Press to seal the edges.
8. Repeat with the remaining rounds and filling. Place on a baking sheet lined with butter paper.
9. You can re-roll the scrap and follow steps 5, 6 and 7 and make patties.
10. Bake in a preheated oven at 350° F for about 30-35 minutes.

Gizzada

Makes: 30-32

Ingredients

<u>Filling:</u>

- 2 cups of water
- 3 cups of brown sugar
- 3 cups of grated coconut
- 2 ounces of butter
- ½ teaspoon of nutmeg

<u>Pastry:</u>

- 4 cups of flour
- 2 teaspoons of shortening
- 1 teaspoon of salt
- 2 teaspoon of butter
- ¾ cup of ice water divided into 3 portions

Method

For the filling:

1. Over low heat, boil the sugar and water to form syrup.
2. Add in the nutmeg and grated coconut to the boiling syrup.
3. Keep stirring the ingredients to prevent it from thickening. Boil for about 15 minutes.
4. Add in the butter. Keep stirring for 6 more minutes. Make sure that the butter melts through the filling and isn't visible.
5. Let the filling cool down completely.

For the pastry:

1. Sift together the salt and flour.
2. Cut the shortening and butter into small chunks and add them to the flour, followed by a third of the ice water. Mix and add another third. Combine and add the last third of the ice water.
3. Form into a pastry dough. Divide the dough into two equal portions. And wrap each with plastic wrap or foil wrap and refrigerate them for 30-40 minutes.
4. Take one portion out of the fridge. Lightly flour a working surface and roll the dough out to roughly ¼" inch of thickness.
5. Using a bowl, glass, or cookie cutter – cut out 16 circles.
6. Crimp each circle to make the casing that will act as the filling's holder.
7. Make sure you crimp in a pattern that is uniform, to get identical and good-looking results.
8. Grease a baking tray. Transfer the casings to the tray and bake them partially for 15 minutes at 350F.
9. Remove them from the oven.
10. Add in the filling to the casings you have baked. Bake for 20 more minutes.
11. Transfer from the oven and allow the Gizzada to cool.
12. Serve hot or warm, and enjoy!
13. Repeat the steps with the second half of the dough resting in the fridge.

Banana Fritters

Makes: 14-16

Ingredients

- 2 and 1/3 cup of mashed bananas, use overripe bananas – 10 medium sized
- ½ teaspoon of nutmeg
- 6 tablespoons of brown sugar
- ½ teaspoon of cinnamon powder
- A pinch or two of salt
- 1 teaspoon of vanilla
- 2 cups of all-purpose flour
- 2 tablespoons of granulated sugar
- 2-3 tablespoons of cooking oil

Method

1. Mash the bananas with the spices and brown sugar. Slowly stir the flour into the banana mash.
2. Heat 2-3 tablespoons of oil in a skillet on high heat, and spoon the batter into the skillet one by one. Make sure you don't overcrowd the skillet.
3. Fry the banana fritter until they are brown and crisp on both the sides. Add more oil if required.
4. If there's no oozing of batter when you press them a little, know that they have cooked through.
5. Transfer the fritters from the skillet to a plate lined with paper towels – to remove the excess oil.
6. Give the fritters a sprinkle of white sugar.
7. Serve warm and enjoy!

Bulla Cakes

Makes: 7-10

Ingredients

- 16 ounces of flour
- ¼ teaspoon baking soda
- ½ teaspoon baking powder
- A couple of pinches of salt
- A couple of pinches of ground nutmeg
- 1 tablespoon of butter
- ½ cup plus 2 tablespoons of brown sugar
- ¼ teaspoon of cinnamon

Method

1. Take the butter and melt it then set it aside for a couple of minutes.
2. Meanwhile, form a syrup with the brown sugar by adding only enough water to help in saturating the sugar.
3. In a mixing bowl, mix all of the dry ingredients and combine them well. Make a crater in the center and pour in the sugar syrup along with the melted butter, and carefully and slowly fold everything together until it comes together like a dough.
4. Preheat the oven to 350F.
5. Lightly flour a working surface and transfer the dough to it and knead for about 5 minutes.

6. Once done, roll the dough out to 1/8" thickness and cut out circles that are 4" wide.
7. Grease a baking sheet and place the circles of dough on it and bake.
8. Bake for around 25 minutes or until the Bullas have risen.

Spice Bun (Loaves)

Makes: 2 loaves

Ingredients

- ½ cup of granulated sugar
- ½ cup of brown sugar
- ½ cup of honey
- 1 tablespoon of molasses
- 2 teaspoons of Caribbean browning sauce
- 2 teaspoons of vanilla
- 2 cups of Guinness Stout
- 8 tablespoons of melted butter
- 2 eggs
- 4 cups of -purpose flour
- 2 cups of dried fruits – raisins and cherries
- 4 teaspoons of baking powder
- 1 tablespoon of cinnamon
- ½ to ¾ teaspoon of salt
- 5 teaspoons of a combination of spices – cinnamon, allspice, and nutmeg
- Optional – 1 cup of cherries to top the loaves with

Method

1. Preheat the oven to 350F. Prepare your loaf tins by greasing them. Set them aside until ready for use.
2. In a large bowl, mix the granulated sugar, brown sugar, browning sauce, honey, melted butter, molasses, egg, vanilla, and the Guinness Stout.
3. In a separate bowl, combine the baking powder, flour, cinnamon, nutmeg, allspice, salt, baking soda, and mix them lightly. Add in the dried fruits.

4. Add the wet ingredients to the dry one and fold the mixture until everything comes together smoothly and there are no lumps left. Avoid over mixing the batter.
5. Pour the batter into the loaf tins equally. Even out the surface. Add the cherries over the top of the batter – optional.
6. Bake for 60 to 75 minutes or until an inserted toothpick or skewer comes out clean.
7. Let the loaves cool down before de-molding or slicing.
8. Enjoy!

Coco Bread

Makes: 5

Ingredients

- 1 tablespoon of instant dry yeast
- 2 cups of all-purpose flour plus ¼ cup while kneading and shaping
- ¼ teaspoon of salt
- 1 tablespoon of sugar
- 2 tablespoon of butter, melted
- 2/3 cup of coconut milk

Method

1. In a bowl, combine the salt, sugar, yeast, and flour. Set it aside.
2. Warm the coconut milk until it is only lukewarm. Avoid heating it anywhere beyond lukewarm or else it will kill the yeast and there will be no rising of the dough. The liquid should always be only slightly warmer than the finger you dip in to check the warmth.
3. Add the melted butter to the lukewarm coconut milk and mix it.
4. Add the wet mixture to the dry one and slowly combine everything until it comes together into a dough until it forms a soft and sticky dough. Add more coconut milk if the dough is too dry. You need a dough that is slightly sticky.

5. Lightly flour a working surface and place the dough on it. Knead it until it feels smooth and elastic.

6. Grease a bowl and place the dough in it. Roll it around once for the dough to get a coating of the oil/butter; this will prevent it from sticking to the bowl.

7. Cover the bowl with a damp cloth or plastic wrap and place it somewhere warm for 60-90 minutes or until the dough has doubled up in size.

8. Preheat the oven to 375F.

9. Lightly flour the working surface and roll the dough out and cut it into small squares to form the individual bread.

10. Form each square into a ball and roll it until it is 1/8" in thickness. Brush the top with some melted butter. Then fold the circle in half, and then fold it in half once again. Repeat this with the rest of the dough.

11. Prepare a baking sheet by lining it with parchment paper and laying the pieces of shaped dough over it. Make sure you place them at least 1-2 inches apart, as they will puff up while baking.

12. Place the baking sheet somewhere warm for around 15 minutes for the dough to rise up.

13. Bake for 15-20 minutes or until the coco bread is golden brown in color.

Chapter Six: Salad Recipes

Mango, Avocado & Cucumber Salad with Scotch Bonnet – Balsamic Herb Vinaigrette

Makes: 8 servings

Ingredients

- 4 mangoes, peeled, pitted, cubed
- 2 cucumbers, peeled, chopped
- 2 avocadoes, peeled, pitted, cubed

For vinaigrette:

- 1 cup olive oil
- 2 teaspoons honey
- 2 tablespoons fresh parsley, finely chopped
- ½ cup balsamic vinegar
- Salt to taste
- Pepper to taste
- 1 scotch bonnet pepper, deseeded

To serve:

- Lettuce leaves

Method

1. To make vinaigrette: Add oil, honey, parsley, vinegar, salt, pepper and scotch bonnet pepper into a blender and blend until smooth.

2. Transfer into a bowl. Cover and set aside in the refrigerator for a couple of hours for the flavors to set in.
3. To make salad: Add all the ingredients of salad into a large bowl and toss well.
4. Pour dressing on top. Toss well.
5. Place lettuce leaves on individual serving plates. Place salad on top and serve.

Jerk Chicken Salad

Makes: 2

Ingredients

- 1 pound leftover Jerk chicken, boneless, skinless – refer Chapter Two – Main dishes
- 1 head romaine lettuce, chopped
- 1 ripe avocado, peeled, pitted, sliced
- 1 cup pineapple chunks
- 1 large red bell pepper, deseeded, cut into rings
- 1 small English cucumber, sliced
- ½ bottle Newman's own Honey Mustard Lite Dressing

Method

1. Place red pepper rings on a preheated grill and grill for 1-2 minutes on each side.
2. Place lettuce leaves on a serving platter. Layer with vegetables and fruits. Place chicken on top.
3. Pour dressing on top. Serve right away.

Green Banana Salad

Makes: 6 servings

Ingredients

- 12 green bananas, trimmed, cut lengthwise
- 1 cup mayonnaise
- 4 green onions, sliced
- 2 cans mixed vegetables
- Salt to taste
- Pepper to taste

Method

1. Place a pot, half filled with water over medium high heat. Add a little salt and bring to the boil. Add bananas and cook until bananas are tender.
2. Remove the bananas with a slotted spoon and place in an ice bath to cool completely.
3. Peel the bananas and cut into pieces. Add into a bowl. Add rest of the ingredients and fold gently.
4. Cover and refrigerate until use.

Avocado Orange Salad

Makes: 10-12 servings

Ingredients

- 12 cups mixed salad greens
- 2 cans Mandarin oranges in light syrup (retain the syrup)
- 2 large avocadoes, peeled, pitted, sliced

For dressing:

- 1 ½ cups oil
- 4 tablespoons red wine vinegar
- 1 cup white vinegar
- ½ cup mayonnaise
- ½ cup retained orange syrup
- 1 teaspoon marjoram

Method

1. To make dressing: Add all the ingredients of the dressing into a blender and blend until smooth.
2. Divide the greens and place on individual serving plates.
3. Layer with orange and avocado slices.
4. Pour dressing on top and serve.

Garden Salad

Makes: 4 servings

Ingredients

- 2 cups cabbage, thinly sliced
- 1 small green bell pepper, cut into rings
- 1 small English cucumber, cut into slices
- 2 carrots, shredded or thinly sliced
- 1 small tomato, cut into wedges
- Thousand Island dressing, as required

Method

1. Add cabbage into a serving bowl. Layer with carrots followed by green bell pepper, cucumber and tomato.
2. Pour dressing on top and serve.

Cabbage Salad

Makes: 2

Ingredients

- 1 small green cabbage, shredded
- 3 stalks celery, chopped
- 2 medium carrots, thinly sliced
- 1 small cucumber, cut into matchsticks
- ¼ cup sugar
- ¼ cup oil
- ¼ cup vinegar
- ½ cup boiling water

Method

1. Add all the ingredients into a bowl and stir. Cover and let it sit for 20 minutes.
2. Drain and serve.

Chapter Seven: Appetizers

Coconut Drops

Makes:

Ingredients

- ½ dry coconut, cut into ¼ inch pieces, rinsed
- ½ tablespoon ginger, grated
- 1 ½ cups water
- ½ pound brown sugar
- A large pinch salt
- ½ teaspoon vanilla extract

Method

1. Add water into a saucepan and place saucepan over high heat.
2. When it begins to boil, add rest of the ingredients and stir. Let it boil for 20-30 minutes.
3. Stir every 3-4 minutes. It will start getting thicker.
4. Grease a baking tray with a little oil. Drop spoonfuls of the mixture over the baking sheet.
5. Cool completely and serve.
6. This can be served as a dessert as well.

Matrimony

Makes: 2-3 servings

Ingredients

- 2 oranges, peeled, separated into segments
- 3 ripe star apples
- 1/8 teaspoon nutmeg, grated
- ½ cup condensed milk.

Method

1. Halve the star apples. Scoop out the pulp along with the seeds first and then discard the seeds.
2. Remove the membrane from the oranges and discard the seeds.
3. Add orange, star apple and condensed milk into a bowl and stir until condensed milk is well coated on the fruits.
4. Spoon into bowls.
5. Garnish with nutmeg and serve.

Grapefruit and Milk

Makes: 4 servings

Ingredients

- 1-2 tablespoons condensed milk
- 1 medium grapefruit, peeled, separated into segments

Method

1. Remove the membrane from the grapefruit and discard the seeds. Cut into pieces
2. Add into a bowl. Add condensed milk and stir until well coated.
3. Spoon into bowls and serve.

Jamaican Carrot Juice

Makes: 3 servings

Ingredients

- 1 pound carrots, scraped, chopped into chunks
- ½ cup condensed milk
- ½ teaspoon vanilla extract
- 2 ½ cups water
- ½ teaspoon nutmeg, finely grated

Method

1. Add carrots into a blender and blend until smooth.
2. Pass the carrot puree through a wire mesh strainer that is placed over a bowl.
3. Discard the pulp. Add condensed milk and vanilla into the bowl of carrot juice.
4. Pour into glasses. Add a bit of nutmeg and swirl with a spoon. Top with crushed ice and serve.

Tropical Guacamole and Plantain Chips

Makes: 12 servings

Ingredients

<u>For tropical guacamole:</u>

- 6 large avocadoes, peeled, pitted, scooped
- 1 -2 cups pineapple, chopped
- 2 cloves garlic, minced
- ½ - 1 cup red onions, minced
- ½ cup fresh cilantro, chopped
- 2 tablespoons extra virgin olive oil
- 1 cup ripe papaya, peeled, deseeded, chopped
- 1 ripe mango, peeled, pitted, chopped
- ½ cup jalapeños, minced
- Lime or lemon juice to taste
- 1 teaspoon ground cumin (optional)
- Salt to taste

<u>For plantain chips:</u>

- 5-6 raw plantains
- Freshly ground pepper to taste
- Seasoned salt or garlic salt to taste
- Oil to fry, as required

Method

1. To make guacamole: Add avocadoes into a large bowl. Mash until chunky. Add lime juice and stir.
2. Add fruits, garlic, onion and cilantro into another bowl and mix well. Transfer into the bowl of avocadoes.

3. Fold gently. Taste and adjust the seasonings if required.

4. To make plantain chips: Peel the plantains and cut into thin slices with a mandolin slicer.

5. Toss plantain slices with salt and paprika. You can either fry or bake in an oven.

6. To bake in an oven: Spread plantain slices on a lined and greased baking sheet, in a single layer. Spray with cooking spray.

7. Bake in a preheated oven at 400° F for about 12- 20 minutes or until crisp. Flip sides half way through baking. Transfer into an airtight container when cooled completely.

8. To make fried plantain chips: Place a skillet over medium high heat. Pour oil to fill up to ½ inch from the bottom of the skillet.

9. Place the skillet over medium heat. Let the oil heat, but it should not smoke.

10. Add chips in batches and fry until brown. Remove with a slotted spoon and place on a plate lined with paper towels. Transfer into an airtight container when cooled completely.

Jerk Shrimp Skewers

Makes: 8 servings

Ingredients

- 3-4 tablespoons Jerk Seasoning blend
- 2 pounds extra-large shrimp (35-40 shrimp), peeled, deveined

For butter sauce:

- ½ cup butter or oil, or more if required
- 1 teaspoon garlic, minced
- 2 tablespoons jerk spice or to taste
- A handful fresh parsley, chopped, to garnish
- Caribbean pepper sauce to taste
- 1 medium onion, sliced

Method

1. If you are using bamboo skewers, then soak in water for 30 minutes.
2. Grease a baking sheet with cooking spray.
3. Add shrimp into a bowl. Sprinkle jerk spice and a little salt and toss well.
4. Insert shrimp on to skewers. Brush oil over it. Place on a baking sheet sprayed with cooking spray.
5. Bake in a preheated oven at 400° F for about 12- 20 minutes or until done.

Tamarind Balls

Makes: 4-6 servings

Ingredients

- 1 cup brown sugar
- ½ cup tamarind paste
- A little water or rum
- Extra sugar to roll

Method

1. Add brown sugar and tamarind flesh into a bowl and mix well. Add water or rum, a bit each time and mix well until the mixture comes together.
2. If the mixture is too watery, add some more sugar. If it is too dry, add some more water or rum.
3. Make balls of the mixture.
4. Place extra sugar on a plate. Dredge the tamarind balls in it. Dredge once more.
5. Serve.

Conclusion

Thank you once again for purchasing this book! I trust it has been to your utmost benefit and a delight to your culinary interests.

You are now fully equipped to not only satisfy your own taste buds with a plethora of Jamaican textures and flavors, but also to impress any friend or family member who hasn't had the opportunity to explore the vast possibilities and horizons of the Jamaican cuisine.

You know for a fact that your kitchen has been calling out to you ever since you read past the first recipe in this book!

Go explore the gastronomical possibilities the Jamaican way.

Finally, if you enjoyed this book, then I'd like to ask you for a favor. Will you be kind enough to leave a review for this book on Amazon? It will be greatly appreciated!

Thank you and good luck!

Other Books by Grizzly Publishing

"Jamaican Cookbook: Traditional Jamaican Recipes Made Easy"

https://www.amazon.com/dp/B07B68KL8D

"Brazilian Instant Pot Cookbook: Delicious Pressure Cooked Meals Made Fast and Easy"

https://www.amazon.com/dp/B078XBYP89

"Norwegian Cookbook: Traditional Scandinavian Recipes Made Easy"

https://www.amazon.com/dp/B079M2W223

"Casserole Cookbook: Delicious Casserole Recipes From Around The World"

https://www.amazon.com/dp/B07B6GV61Q

Lightning Source UK Ltd.
Milton Keynes UK
UKHW031245111120
373211UK00003B/306